Exam Success in
Chemistry
for Cambridge IGCSE®
Practical Workbook

T0347623

Primrose Kitten

OXFORD
UNIVERSITY PRESS

OXFORD
UNIVERSITY PRESS

Great Clarendon Street, Oxford, OX2 6DP, United Kingdom

Oxford University Press is a department of the University of Oxford. It furthers the University's objective of excellence in research, scholarship, and education by publishing worldwide. Oxford is a registered trade mark of Oxford University Press in the UK and in certain other countries

British Library Cataloguing in Publication Data
Data available

978-1-38-200638-5

3 5 7 9 10 8 6 4 2

The manufacturing process conforms to the environmental regulations of the country of origin.

Printed in Great Britain by Bell and Bain Ltd, Glasgow

Acknowledgements

®IGCSE is the registered trademark of Cambridge International Examinations.

The publisher and authors would like to thank the following for permission to use photographs and other copyright material:

Cover: Ruslana Bat/Shutterstock Images.

Artwork by Q2A Media Services Pvt. Ltd.; Six Red Marbles; Aptara; Peter Banks; Green Gate Publishing Services; Thomson Digital and Pantek Arts Ltd.; Oxford Designers and Illustrators Ltd.; IFA Design, Plymouth, UK; Clive Goodyer; Phoenix Photosetting; Nelson Thornes Ltd.; Vijay; Tech Set Ltd. Gateshead; OUPC and OUP.

Every effort has been made to contact copyright holders of material reproduced in this book. Any omissions will be rectified in subsequent printings if notice is given to the publisher.

Links to third party websites are provided by Oxford in good faith and for information only. Oxford disclaims any responsibility for the materials contained in any third party website referenced in this work.

This Practical Workbook refers to the Cambridge IGCSE® Chemistry (0620) and Cambridge O Level Chemistry (5070) Syllabuses published by Cambridge Assessment International Education.

This work has been developed independently from and is not endorsed by or otherwise connected with Cambridge Assessment International Education.

Introduction

Experimental skills and investigations make up 20% of the assessment weighting in Cambridge IGCSE® and are examined in Papers 5 and 6. This book will help students prepare for the practical exams. Students being able to recall the practicals they have studied in class will not be enough to get the marks. They need to be able to adapt that knowledge to new situations; find errors in practicals; plan and improve practicals. This workbook is designed to fully prepare students for success in these exams.

The exam success practical workbook:
- covers the practical skills needed for Papers 5 and 6
- allows students to develop their experimental skills
- provides a wide range of test questions to assess performance in practicals.

Contents

1	Simple quantitative experiments in chemistry	5
2	Rates of reaction	8
3	Salt preparation	14
4	Separation and purification techniques	17
5	Electrolysis	23
6	Identification of metal ions, non-metal ions and gases	27
7	Chemical tests for water	31
8	Test-tube reactions of dilute acids	32
9	Tests for oxidising and reducing agents	33
10	Heating and cooling curves	34
11	Titrations	36
12	Solubility	41
13	Melting points and boiling points	43
14	Displacement reactions of metals and halogens	47
15	Temperature changes during reactions	50
16	Metals corroding	54
Glossary		58
Periodic table		59
Common ions		60
General equations		61
Common simple molecules		62
Answers		63
Notes		70

1. A new student is being introduced to measuring volumes in chemistry.

   a. Which image correctly shows how a pipette is filled?

   .... [1]

   b. A student read the value on pipette A as 0.00 cm^3. This is incorrect.

      i. Give the correct reading on pipette A.

      .... [1]

      ii. Name the type of **error** that has been introduced with a reading of 0.00 cm^3.

      .... [1]

      iii. Calculate the difference between the volume of liquid in pipettes A and B.

      ....

      .... [1]

   c. A student is carrying out a **titration** with potassium manganate(V) solution in the burette. As potassium manganate(V) is dark purple, they cannot use the usual method for reading the volume of liquid in the burette. Instead he reads the volume from the top of the meniscus. Explain why this will still lead to accurate titrations.

   ....

   .... [2]

2. A student is measuring the volume of gas released when magnesium reacts with an acid. They collect the gas in an inverted measuring cylinder.

   a. Give the reading for the volume of gas collected in the set-up shown in the figure.

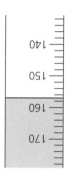

   .... [1]

   b. The results of the experiment are shown below. Draw a table to show these results.

Time / minutes	0	2	4	6	8	10	12
Water level in measuring cylinder	0–5–10	10–15–20	25–30–35	25–30–35	35–40–45	40–45–50	40–45–50

[4]

3. A student is measuring the volume of gas released at different times during an experiment. They draw the following graph to show their results.

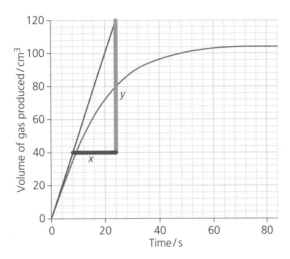

a. Give the total time that the experiment ran for.

.... [1]

b. Determine how much gas had been produced by 20 s after the start of the experiment.

.... [1]

c. The student wants to determine the rate of reaction at 0 s. They have drawn a tangent to the graph at this time. The gradient of the tangent will give the rate of reaction at 0 s.

   i. Calculate the rate of reaction at 0 s by finding the change in volume of gas produced divided by the change in time.

   ....

   ....

   .... [3]

   ii. Give the final volume of gas produced.

   .... [1]

1. A student is investigating rates of reaction by measuring the production of a gas.

   Method

   Measuring the production of a gas

   Step 1 Fill the trough and the measuring cylinder with water, and clamp the cylinder upside down in the trough.

   Step 2 Set up the conical flask, bung and delivery tube so that the exit of the delivery tube is under the measuring cylinder.

   Step 3 Add 50 cm³ of 2 mol/dm³ hydrochloric acid into the conical flask.

   Step 4 Sandpaper 3 cm of magnesium ribbon and drop it into the conical flask. Quickly replace the bung, and start the stopwatch.

   Step 5 Record the volume of gas produced every 10 seconds until no more gas is being produced.

   Step 6 Repeat Steps 1 to 5, for each concentration of hydrochloric acid.

   Exam tip

   There are several different methods for finding rates of reaction. However, the same principles are applicable to all of them.

   The method of collecting gas with an inverted measuring cylinder is similar to the method for investigating photosynthesis in biology.

   This is a favourite practical question of examiners – learn it well!

   a. Name the **dependent variable** in this experiment.

   .... [1]

   b. State the concentration of the acid used in this method.

   .... [1]

   c. List **three control variables** that have been used.

   ....

   ....

   .... [3]

   d. List **three** other ways (apart from the one given in this method) that can be used to follow a rate of reaction.

   ....

   ....

   .... [3]

   e. Magnesium ribbon slowly reacts with the oxygen in the air to form magnesium oxide. This coats any magnesium ribbon in a dull white/grey layer. Explain why it is important to rub the magnesium ribbon with sandpaper before use.

   ....

   .... [2]

f. Hydrogen gas is released during the reaction between hydrochloric acid and magnesium ribbon. Describe a test for hydrogen gas.

....

.... [1]

g. Identify which of the following equations is correct. Tick **one** box. [1]

mean rate of reaction = quantity of product formed ÷ time taken ☐

mean rate of reaction = time taken ÷ quantity of product formed ☐

mean rate of reaction = quantity of product formed × time taken ☐

mean rate of reaction = quantity of reactant used × time taken ☐

h. A student carries out this experiment. They measure $56\,dm^3$ of gas produced in 15 seconds. Calculate the mean **rate of reaction**. Give your answer correct to 2 significant figures. Include the unit with your answer.

Exam tip

Don't forget to state the units.

....

....

.... [3]

2. A student reacts marble chips with hydrochloric acid and collects the gas produced in a syringe.

    a. She wants to investigate the effect of concentration on the rate of reaction. She records the volume of gas in the syringe every 5 seconds. She repeats the experiment three times using different concentrations of hydrochloric acid:

       $0.5\,mol/dm^3$ HCl

       $1.0\,mol/dm^3$ HCl

       $2.0\,mol/dm^3$ HCl

       Predict how the results would vary for the three concentrations of acid.

       ....

       ....

       ....

       ....

       ....

       ....

       ....

       .... [3]

    b. The student then investigates the effect of temperature on the rate of reaction. She keeps the concentration of acid the same but changes the temperature. She draws the following graph of her results.

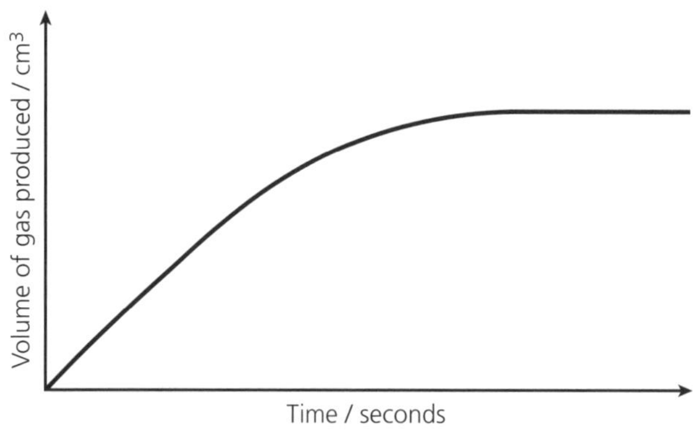

       The student then repeats the experiment at a higher temperature.

      i. Sketch a line on the graph to show the results you would predict at a higher temperature. [2]

      ii. Explain your prediction.

       ....

       ....

       ....

       .... [3]

3. A student reacts marble chips with hydrochloric acid in a flask. He places the flask on a balance and records the mass at different times. His results are shown in the table.

Time / s	0	10	20	30	40
Mass of flask / g	95	43	27	21	20

a. i. Plot the student's results on the grid below. [4]

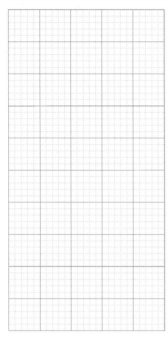

ii. Draw a **line of best fit** on the graph. [1]

iii. Compare the rate of reaction at 10 seconds with the rate at 30 seconds.

....

.... [2]

b. i. Write the equation to calculate the mean rate of reaction in g/s.

.... [1]

ii. Calculate the mean rate of reaction in g/s between 0 s and 40 s.

....

.... [2]

iii. Calculate the rate of reaction at 10 s in g/s.

....

.... [2]

iv. Calculate the rate of reaction at 10 s in mol/s.

....

.... [2]

> **Exam tip**
>
> If you are asked about the rate at a point on a curved graph, you need to draw a tangent to the curve at that point. Remember: the steeper the tangent, the faster the rate.

> **Exam tip**
>
> You are simply being asked to convert g/s into mol/s. This is the same as converting grams to moles of a substance. Think about what substance is being lost from the container. What is its relative formula mass?

4. A student is measuring the rate of reaction by change in turbidity using the following method.

Method

Measuring reaction rate by change in turbidity

Step 1 Add sodium thiosulfate solution and distilled water to a conical flask in the proportions shown in the table to make each concentration.

Volume of distilled water / cm^3	40	30	20	10	0
Volume of sodium thiosulfate / cm^3	10	20	30	40	50
Final sodium thiosulfate concentration / g/dm^3	8	16	24	32	40

Step 2 Collect a printed cross from the teacher.

Step 3 Add $10\,cm^3$ dilute hydrochloric acid to one of the conical flasks and place the conical flask on the black cross. Start the stopwatch.

Step 4 Record the time when the black cross is no longer visible.

Step 5 Repeat Steps 3–4 for the other concentrations of sodium thiosulfate.

a. After the first three concentrations, they lose the printed cross that the teacher had provided. They decide to draw their own cross on a piece of paper instead of getting another printed copy from their teacher. Comment on their decision.

....

....

.... [2]

b. The reaction between hydrochloric acid and sodium thiosulfate can be described by the following equation. Balance this equation by writing numbers on the dotted lines. [2]

$$......HCl(aq) + Na_2S_2O_3(aq) \rightarrow ......NaCl(aq) + S(s) + SO_2(g) + H_2O(l)$$

c. The reaction between hydrochloric acid and sodium thiosulfate produces products in different states. Give the state of each of the following products and what the student observes.

i. S .... [2]

ii. NaCl .... [1]

iii. SO_2 .... [2]

5. A group of students are carrying out two experiments on rates of reaction. Explain why it is important to have the same person doing the same job, when…

a. noting the time at which the cross disappears

.... [1]

b. adding the magnesium ribbon to the hydrochloric acid and putting the bung into the flask.

.... [1]

6. A group of students is investigating the reaction between hydrochloric acid and sodium thiosulfate. They keep the volumes of the reactants the same but change the temperature.

    a. Name the **independent variable** in this experiment.

    .... [1]

    b. When the group of students carry out this experiment, they cannot agree on the time at which the cross disappears. Suggest an alternative method that would give more accurate data.

    .... [1]

    c. The students investigate the effect of changing the concentration of the sodium thiosulfate. When increasing the volume of sodium thiosulfate in the reaction mixture, the volume of water added decreases. Explain why this is important.

    ....

    .... [1]

    d. The concentration of sodium thiosulfate has been given as $40\,g/dm^3$. Explain what this means.

    ....

    .... [1]

1. A student is preparing a pure, dry sample of a salt by reacting an insoluble metal oxide with a dilute acid using the following method.

   Step 1   Using a measuring cylinder, measure 20 cm^3 of dilute sulfuric acid into a beaker.

   Step 2   Add half a spatula of copper oxide into the dilute sulfuric acid and stir with the glass rod.

   Step 3   Warm the beaker and its contents gently. Do not allow the reacting mixture to boil.

   Step 4   Continue adding the copper oxide in small amounts until no more dissolves (this should be most of the solid you have been provided with).

   Step 5   Set up a filter funnel and filter paper in a conical flask. Filter the mixture and discard the unreacted copper oxide.

   Step 6   Pour the filtrate into an evaporating basin and place it over a beaker of water. Heat the water until the volume of the solution in the evaporating basin is halved.

   Step 7   Remove from the heat. When cool, stand the evaporating basin on a piece of paper. Leave it overnight to crystallise.

   Step 8   The following day, remove the crystals from the concentrated solution with a spatula and gently pat them dry between two pieces of filter paper.

   a. Sketch and label a diagram to show the set-up in Step 5.

   [6]

   b. Identify the hazards in this practical, describe the risks associated with them and suggest what can be done to prevent each risk happening.

   ....

   ....

   ....

   ....

   ....

   .... [6]

Exam tip

You can be asked about the method to produce any salt, not just the ones you're familiar with. You need to learn all of the general salt equations and be able to apply them:

metal + acid → salt + hydrogen
metal oxide + acid → salt + water
metal hydroxide + acid → salt + water
metal carbonate + acid →
                salt + water + carbon dioxide

Using hydrochloric acid will lead to the production of chloride salts.
Using sulfuric acid will lead to the production of sulfate salts.
Using nitric acid will lead to the production of nitrate salts.

To help you to work out the formula of the salt, it is important to learn the formulae and charges for all the common ions.

Exam tip

Think about what can harm you, how it can harm you and how you can prevent it from harming you.

c. Suggest the function of the filter paper in Step 5.

.... [1]

d. Step 6 involves putting the evaporating basin over a water bath and heating so that the water evaporates.

   Suggest **one** other method of evaporating the water.

   .... [1]

e. Describe the purpose of evaporating the water.

   .... [1]

f. Suggest why it is important that the copper oxide is added in excess in Step 4.

   .... [1]

g. The equation for the reaction is

$$CuO + H_2SO_4 \rightarrow CuSO_4 + H_2O$$

Calculate the mass of copper sulfate produced from 17 g of copper oxide.

Relative atomic mass of Cu = 63.5
Relative atomic mass of O = 16
Relative atomic mass of S = 32
Relative atomic mass of H = 1

mass of copper sulfate produced = ... g [3]

2. Hydrochloric acid reacts with magnesium or magnesium carbonate.
   Both magnesium and magnesium carbonate give magnesium chloride as one product and a gas as the other product:
   magnesium + hydrochloric acid → magnesium chloride + gas A
   magnesium carbonate + hydrochloric acid → magnesium chloride + water + gas B
   Identify gas A and gas B and describe the test to confirm the identity of each gas.

   Gas A is ....

   Test for gas A: ....

   ....

   Gas B is ....

   Test for gas B: ....

   .... [4]

3. Calcium sulfate is produced in the following reaction:

$$H_2SO_4(aq) + Ca(OH)_2(aq) \rightarrow CaSO_4(s) + 2H_2O(l)$$

A student carried out this reaction. Explain what they observe.

....

.... [2]

4. A salt is a compound formed when an acid reacts with a base. Write a word equation for the production of each of the following salts:

Exam tip
It is important that you can apply any of the general salt equations.

a. potassium chloride

....

.... [2]

b. iron sulfate

....

.... [2]

c. lead nitrate.

....

.... [2]

1. Filtration

a. Label parts A–D in the diagram. [4]

A.............................
B.............................
C.............................
D.............................

b. Explain what filtration can be used to separate and what it cannot separate.

....

....

....

.... [3]

2. Crystallisation

evaporating basin   copper(II) sulfate solution

heat

solution from evaporating basin

cold tile

leave for a few days to crystallise

a. A student made a **saturated solution** of copper(II) sulfate.

i. Define the term saturated solution.

....

.... [2]

ii. Explain what will be left in the evaporating basin after crystallisation.

....

.... [1]

iii. State how a student could change the mass of salt needed to make a saturated solution.

.... [1]

b. A student evaporates the solution using a Bunsen burner. Another student leaves the evaporating basin on the window sill for a few days. Describe the differences in the crystals that the two students obtain.

....

....

....

.... [3]

3. **Simple distillation**

   Method

   Step 1   Set up the apparatus as shown in the diagram.

   Step 2   Adjust the height of the thermometer so that the bulb is in line with the opening of the delivery tube.

   Step 3   Light the Bunsen burner with the air hole closed.

   Step 4   Open the air hole of the Bunsen burner so that the flame turns blue and move the Bunsen burner under the tripod to heat the solution.

   Step 5   Note the temperature on the thermometer when it is at a constant value. This is the boiling point of the distillate.

   Step 6   Once half a boiling tube of distillate has been collected, remove the delivery tube and turn off the Bunsen burner.

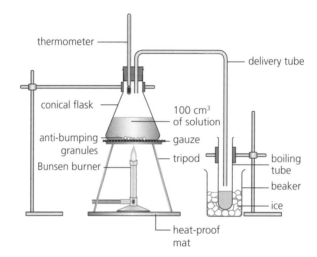

a. List the hazards in this experiment and describe how students can keep themselves safe.

   ....

   ....

   ....

   .... [4]

b. A student carries out the experiment. The solution started to boil at 100 °C. Identify this solution.

   .... [1]

c. Name an item of equipment that could be used to measure 100 cm³ of solution.

   .... [1]

d. Give the function of the ice.

   ....

   .... [2]

e. After the distillation, identify what will be left in the conical flask.

   .... [1]

f. A student labels two solutions A and B but forgets to write down which one is which. They know that the two solutions are:

Exam tip

Don't do more calculations than necessary. The solutions have the same concentration, so you only need to compare their relative formula mass.

- 1 mol/dm³ sodium chloride (NaCl)

- 1 mol/dm³ sodium hydrogen carbonate (NaHCO₃).

After evaporating the water, sample A was found to contain 0.585 g of salt and sample B contained 0.84 g of salt.

i. Identify which sample is 0.5 mol/dm³ sodium hydrogen carbonate. Explain how you know.

....

....

.... [3]

ii. Suggest another way of identifying the two solutions that doesn't require the liquid to be evaporated.

.... [1]

4. Fractional distillation

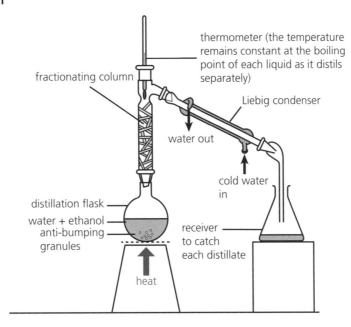

thermometer (the temperature remains constant at the boiling point of each liquid as it distils separately)

fractionating column

Liebig condenser

water out

cold water in

distillation flask
water + ethanol
anti-bumping granules

receiver to catch each distillate

heat

Simple **fractional distillation** can be carried out in the laboratory using the equipment shown.

The boiling point of water is 100 °C. The boiling point of ethanol is 78 °C. Both are colourless liquids. Describe a method you could use to separate a mixture of 25% ethanol and 75% water.

....

....

....

....

....

.... [6]

5. **Chromatography**

   Method

   Step 1 Use a pencil to draw a horizontal origin line, 1 cm from the bottom of the **chromatography** paper.

   Step 2 Use a pencil to draw a cross on the centre of the origin line.

   Step 3 Use a thin paint brush or capillary tube to add some of the food colouring onto the cross and allow it to dry.

   Step 4 Fold the top edge of the chromatography paper over a wooden splint and keep in place with a paper clip.

   Step 5 Add water to a depth of 0.5 cm into the beaker.

   Step 6 Carefully lower the chromatography paper into the beaker, taking care to keep the pencil line above the water level. Leave until the water line (solvent front) has passed the last coloured spot.

   Step 7 Remove the **chromatogram** and allow it to dry.

   a. Explain why it is important to draw the origin line in pencil.

   ....

   .... [2]

   b. Explain where the solvent should be, in relation to the origin line, at the start of the practical.

   ....

   .... [2]

   c. Explain why a lid might be needed in this experiment.

   .... [1]

   d. A capillary tube is used to make small dots of the sample. This needs to be done carefully to stop the spots touching each other. Describe why it is important to have separate spots of each sample.

   .... [1]

   e. To calculate the R_f value, you need to measure the distance of the spot from the origin line. State where on the spot you should take the measurement from.

   .... [1]

   f. Two groups of students carry out a chromatography practical task. Group A allows the solvent to move up until it reaches $\frac{3}{4}$ of the way up the paper. Group B lets the experiment run until the solvent has reached the top of the paper. Comment on these two methods and explain which will give more accurate results.

   ....

   ....

   .... [3]

   g. Describe why it is important to ensure that the sides of the paper do not touch the sides of the beaker.

   .... [1]

   h. State and explain whether chromatography is a **qualitative** or a **quantitative** technique.

   ....

   .... [2]

i. For the sample to move up the paper, it must dissolve in the solvent. Describe what you would see if a soluble sample was compared with an insoluble sample.

....

.... [2]

j. Complete the diagram using the terms in the box. [4]

solvent	solvent front	R_f value = 0.34	R_f value = 0.60

k. Chromatography can be used to test whether certain known substances are present in a sample. Five different food colouring samples (A–E) are compared to red, blue and yellow reference samples. The results are shown.

i. Use evidence from the diagram to suggest which colour is sample B.

.... [1]

ii. State how many different substances make up sample A.

.... [1]

iii. Give the letters of two unknown samples that are actually the same mixture.

.... [2]

iv. Use a ruler to draw a line on the diagram showing where the solvent should be in relation to the origin line at the start of the experiment. [1]

I. a. Use the diagram to determine which **two** athletes have been using banned substances.

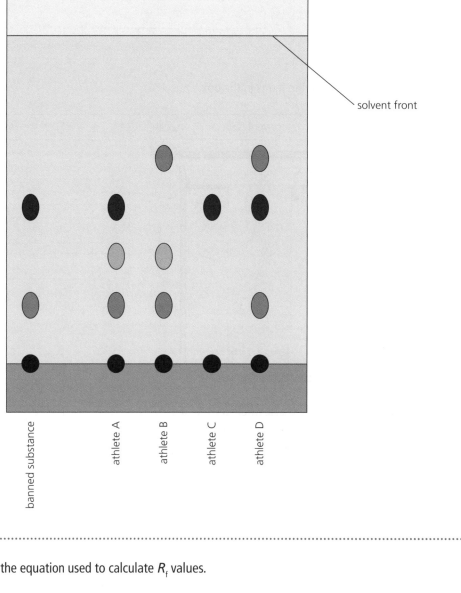

.... [2]

b. i. Write the equation used to calculate R_f values.

....

.... [1]

ii. Calculate the R_f value of the spot in sample C.

....

.... [1]

1. A student is investigating the **electrolysis** of copper chloride using the following method.

Method for the electrolysis of copper chloride

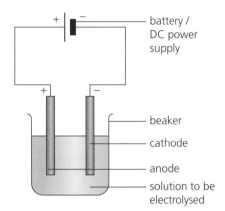

Exam tip

There are many examples of solutions that can undergo electrolysis. You need to be able to apply the basic principles to these examples. You need to be able to predict the products, identify which electrode each ion goes to and write equations for the reaction at each electrode.

Step 1   Pour 50 cm³ copper(II) chloride solution into a 100 cm³ beaker.

Step 2   Insert two carbon **electrodes** into the solution, ensuring that they do not touch.

Step 3   Attach the electrodes to the DC power supply using leads and crocodile clips.

Step 4   Switch on the power supply at 4 V and carefully observe what happens at the **anode** and the **cathode**. Record your observations.

Step 5   Position a piece of damp litmus paper above the solution next to the anode. Record your observations.

Step 6   Collect a new set of electrodes, wash the equipment and repeat Steps 1–5 with 50 cm³ sodium chloride solution in the beaker.

a. List the equipment needed to carry out the method above.

....

....

....

....

.... [5]

b. A student set up this experiment and was careful not to let the electrode rods touch each other. Describe the effect of letting the electrodes touch each other.

....

....

.... [2]

c. Describe what safety precautions should be taken during the electrolysis of copper(II) chloride.

....

....

....

....

....

.... [6]

d. Two students carried out this experiment. One followed the instructions carefully and ran the experiment at 4 V, while the other ran the experiment at 1 V. Compare the results of the two experiments.

Exam tip

When **compare** is the command word, you need to state what is the same and what is different.

....

....

....

.... [4]

e. After carefully setting up the experiment, a student did not see any gas coming from the electrodes. Suggest a way of altering the experimental set-up that would show whether the circuit is working properly.

....

....

.... [2]

f. The positive and negative electrodes have names. Complete these statements.

   i. The cathode is the .... electrode. [1]

   ii. The anode is the .... electrode. [1]

g. Copper ions and sodium ions both go to the same electrode.

   i. State which electrode this is.

   .... [1]

   ii. Explain why copper ions and sodium ions both go to the same electrode.

   ....

   ....

   .... [2]

h. Copper(II) chloride and copper sulfate both release gases at the positive electrode. For each compound, name the gas that is released and describe how to test for this gas.

    i. Copper chloride

       Gas released: ....

       Test for gas: ....

       .... [2]

    ii. Copper sulfate

       Gas released: ....

       Test for gas: ....

       .... [2]

i. Describe what happens when copper ions reach the negative electrode.

....

....

.... [3]

j. In the electrolysis of sodium chloride, two gases are released at the different electrodes. Hydrogen gas is formed at one electrode. Explain why this gas is formed instead of sodium metal.

.... [1]

k. There are three products from the electrolysis of sodium chloride: two gases and a solution. Give the formula of the solution.

.... [1]

l. Sodium chloride is used in its solid form as a food additive, namely, salt. Explain why solid sodium chloride cannot undergo electrolysis.

....

....

.... [2]

m. When sodium chloride undergoes electrolysis, two gases are released from a colourless solution. Explain how the **pH** of the solution changes when these gases are released.

.... [1]

n. State the difference between **oxidation** and **reduction**.

.... [1]

o. Write **ionic half equations** to describe what happens at each electrode during the electrolysis of copper(II) chloride.

....

....

....

....

....

.... [6]

Exam tip

Look at the number of marks available for each question. 6 marks doesn't mean that you need to write an essay, but you do need to write **three** things about each electrode.

6 Identification of metal ions, non-metal ions and gases

Methods for identification of metal and non-metal ions

Flame tests

Step 1 Put a clean, dry nichrome wire loop into a blue Bunsen flame to ensure that the loop is clean.

Step 2 Put the clean loop into the sample mixture.

Step 3 Put the loop back into the blue Bunsen flame and note the colour.

Metal ion precipitation test

Step 1 Add two drops of the solution to be tested into a dimple.

Step 2 Then add two drops of sodium hydroxide solution.

Step 3 Note the colour of the **precipitate**.

Carbonate test

Step 1 Half fill a test tube with **limewater** and put it in a test-tube rack.

Step 2 Half fill a second test tube with the solution to be tested, and mount at a 45° angle using the stand, boss and clamp.

Step 3 Add 2 cm³ dilute hydrochloric acid and quickly insert a bung and a delivery tube so any gas produced bubbles through the limewater.

Step 4 Observe to see whether the limewater goes cloudy.

Sulfate test

Step 1 Add two drops of the solution to be tested into a dimple.

Step 2 Then add two drops of dilute hydrochloric acid and two drops of barium chloride solution.

Step 3 If a white precipitate forms, the sample contains sulfate ions.

Halide test

Step 1 Add two drops of the solution to be tested into a dimple.

Step 2 Then add two drops of nitric acid solution and two drops of silver nitrate solution. Note the colour of any precipitate formed.

1. Complete the table to give the different colours obtained with a flame test. [5]

Positive ion	lithium	sodium	potassium	calcium	copper
Flame test colour					

2. A student is testing an unknown sample and thinks it is sodium sulfate. Describe the observations that would confirm the presence of sodium and sulfate ions.

....

....

....

....

.... [4]

3. Give the formula for a sulfate ion.

    .... [1]

4. Hydrochloric acid and nitric acid are used when testing for negative ions. Give the formula of each of these acids.

    hydrochloric acid .... [1]

    nitric acid .... [1]

Exam tip

Remember that the size and positioning of your numbers and letters is really important when giving the formula for an ion.

5. The test for carbon dioxide is to see whether a gas turns limewater cloudy, while the test for oxygen is to see whether a gas relights a glowing splint. Give an alternative test for carbon dioxide using a splint.

    .... [1]

Exam tip

Make sure that you use all the information in the question.

6. To identify the positive ion that a solution contains, a student used a wire loop and carried out a flame test. Suggest alternative equipment for carrying out flame tests on solutions.

    .... [1]

7. When testing metal ions with sodium hydroxide, the products include a metal hydroxide. Copper(I) hydroxide and copper(II) hydroxide have different formulae as do iron(II) hydroxide and iron(III) hydroxide. Give the formula for each compound and state the result of testing each metal ion with sodium hydroxide.

    a. Copper(I) hydroxide

        Formula: .... [1]

    b. Copper(II) hydroxide

        Formula: .... [1]

        Result with sodium hydroxide: .... [1]

    c. Iron(II) hydroxide

        Formula: .... [1]

        Result with sodium hydroxide: .... [1]

    d. Iron(III) hydroxide

        Formula: .... [1]

        Result with sodium hydroxide: .... [1]

8. A student carries out a series of flame tests and finds that every sample he tests contains sodium. This is not the correct result. Suggest what has happened to give the incorrect results and how the student could alter his method to ensure that this does not happen again.

   ....

   ....

   ....

   .... [3]

9. To test a gas to find out whether it is carbon dioxide (CO_2), the gas is bubbled though limewater ($Ca(OH)_2$). If it is carbon dioxide, then the limewater will go cloudy.

   a. Write a balanced symbol equation for the reaction between carbon dioxide and limewater (calcium hydroxide).

   .... [2]

   b. Explain why the limewater goes cloudy.

   .... [1]

10. Calcium ions, magnesium ions and aluminium ions all form a white precipitate when sodium hydroxide is added.

    Exam tip

    This question is asking for an ionic equation, so the charges on each side have to be balanced as well as the number of moles of each element.

    a. Write a balanced ionic equation for the addition of hydroxide to calcium ions.

    .... [2]

    b. Describe how sodium hydroxide can be used to determine whether a sample contains magnesium ions or aluminium ions.

    ....

    .... [1]

    c. Describe how a student could differentiate between magnesium ions and calcium ions in a sample.

    ....

    .... [2]

11. Two students test a sample for halide ions. One student thinks that the test gives a positive result for bromide ions and the second student thinks that the results indicate the presence of iodide ions. Describe how the students could confirm their results. You should include a description of the expected positive result for each ion.

    ....

    ....

    ....

    ....

    .... [5]

12. A student wants to identify the negative ion in a sample. First, she tests the sample for sulfate ions. This test gives a negative result. Then she tests the **same** sample for halide ions. This test gives a positive result. However, this is a false positive result as the sample actually contains carbonate ions. Identify the error the student has made and explain why this gives a false positive result.

....

.... [2]

13. For each of the following samples, describe which tests would give positive results and what would be observed.

a. lithium chloride

....

....

....

.... [4]

b. sodium carbonate

....

....

....

.... [4]

c. copper sulfate

....

....

....

.... [4]

14. The science preparation room at a school flooded and the labels came off three of the bottles of chemicals. The teacher asked the class to identify the substances in these bottles. The results are as follows.

Sample A gave off a gas when heated, which turned limewater cloudy. Samples A and B both gave a white precipitate when tested with sodium hydroxide. The precipitate didn't dissolve when excess sodium hydroxide was added. Sample C gave a white precipitate when mixed with nitric acid and silver nitrate, while sample B gave a white precipitate when mixed with hydrochloric acid and barium chloride. Sample A gave an orange flame test while sample C gave a crimson flame test.

Identify the three samples.

Exam tip

Highlighter pens are useful for this type of long, wordy question. Either highlight all the information about each sample in one colour (e.g. sample A in pink, sample B in blue) or highlight all the positive ion test results in one colour and the negative results in another. You can cross out information once you've dealt with it.

Sample A is ....

Sample B is ....

Sample C is .... [6]

1. A student has obtained a saturated solution of copper(II) sulfate. She wants to produce blue crystals. She evaporates the solution by heating it vigorously. Small white crystals are left in the bottom of the dish.

   a. Name the small white crystals in the dish.

   .... [1]

   b. Suggest how the student can convert these small white crystals to blue copper(II) sulfate crystals.

   .... [1]

   c. Write a word equation for the reaction in **b**.

   .... [2]

2. A student has two clear liquids. He knows that one of the solutions is water and the other is ethanoic acid (vinegar). Describe **two** different methods that the student could use to differentiate between these two colourless liquids.

   ....

   ....

   ....

   ....

   ....

   ....

   .... [7]

1. A student reacts calcium carbonate with dilute hydrochloric acid. They observe that a gas is evolved.

   a. Name this gas and describe how its identity can be confirmed.

   ....

   .... [2]

   b. This gas is just one of three products obtained in this reaction. List the other two products.

   ....

   .... [2]

2. A student places strips of magnesium and zinc into separate test tubes containing dilute hydrochloric acid.

   a. Describe what the student observes in each test tube.

   ....

   ....

   .... [3]

   b. Magnesium and zinc both react with dilute hydrochloric acid to form a gas. Identify this gas.

   .... [1]

   c. Give the test for this gas.

   .... [1]

3. A student has two identical beakers that contain colourless solutions. Neither of the beakers is labelled. The student knows that one contains a base and the other contains an acid.

   The student tests the solutions in three ways and records their results in a table.

   a. Complete the results table.

	litmus	thymolphthalein	methyl orange
Expected result with acid			
Expected result with alkali			
Expected result with neutral solution			

   b. Suggest why it is necessary to test the unknown liquids with both thymolphthalein and methyl orange.

   .... [1]

   c. Give an alternative way of measuring the pH of the solutions that would give a clearer answer about their identities.

   .... [1]

9 Tests for oxidising and reducing agents

1. A student wants to find out whether or not a compound is a reducing agent.

   a. Complete table.

Compound	Reducing agent	Oxidising agent
potassium iodide		
nitric acid		
carbon		
hydrogen		
acidified potassium manganate(VII)		
oxygen		

   [6]

   b. Name the type of compound that should be used to determine whether or not a substance is a **reducing agent**.

   .... [1]

   c. The student tested a colourless solution containing iron(II) ions and observed a colour change from purple to colourless. Explain the reason for the colour change.

   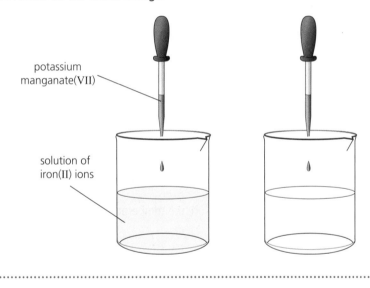

   potassium manganate(VII)

   solution of iron(II) ions

   ....

   .... [2]

   d. The student wrote the following equation for the reaction:

   $$MnO_4^-(aq) + 8H^+(aq) + 5e^- \rightarrow Mn^{2+}(aq) + 4H_2O(l)$$

   Use this equation to help you to complete these sentences.

   i. The purple manganate ion is ....

   ii. The colourless manganate ion is .... [1]

   e. Give the expected colour change when potassium iodide is used to test for an **oxidising agent**.

   .... [1]

1. A student is investigating ice turning into steam and draws the heating curve.

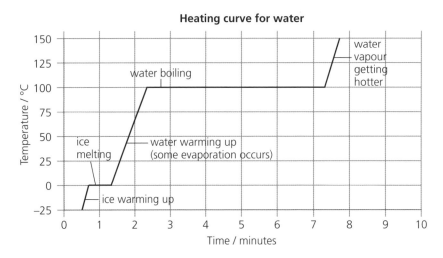

Heating curve for water

a. State the duration of the experiment.

.... [2]

b. Give the temperature at which the sample turned from a liquid into a gas.

.... [1]

c. The student suspected that the sample might not be pure. Use data from the graph to support or disprove this suspicion.

....

.... [2]

d. Name the equipment that can be used to measure the temperature of the water.

.... [1]

e. Give the time for which the water was boiling.

.... [2]

f. Suggest **four** safety precautions that a student should take when carrying out this experiment.

....

Exam tip

Notice the different temperatures in the experiment.

....

....

.... [4]

g. The student measures the time taken for the water to turn into steam in minutes. Explain why this is the best unit to use and why seconds or hours would not have been appropriate.

....

....

....

.... [4]

2. A student draws the curve.

a. Identify the type of curve that the student has drawn.

.... [1]

b. Give the boiling point of the compound.

.... [1]

c. Describe what happens at 17 °C.

....

.... [2]

d. Suggest an improvement that the student could make to the graph.

.... [1]

3. A student is given this graph.

a. The student thinks that this is the **cooling curve** for water. State whether or not this is a correct statement. Explain how you decide.

....

.... [2]

b. Name the process taking place when a liquid turns into a solid.

.... [1]

Exam tip

Don't forget to use data from the graph.

c. The boiling point of this compound was 53 °C. Give the condensing point of the compound.

.... [1]

35

1. A student is carrying out a titration to find the volume of acid that will be neutralised by an alkali, using the method shown below.

   Step 1 Collect some dilute sulfuric acid in a labelled beaker.

   Step 2 Fill a burette with the dilute sulfuric acid just beyond the zero, and then let the solution run out until the bottom of the meniscus is exactly on zero.

   Step 3 Collect 0.100 mol/dm³ sodium hydroxide solution in another labelled beaker.

   Step 4 Use a 25.0 cm³ pipette and pipette filler to transfer 25.0 cm³ of the sodium hydroxide into a clean, dry conical flask.

   Step 5 Add three to four drops of phenolphthalein **indicator** into the flask and swirl. Place the conical flask on a white tile directly below the burette.

   Step 6 Record the initial burette reading in a suitable results table.

   Step 7 Carry out a rough titration by adding the acid to the alkali in small amounts at a time. Swirl the flask after every addition and continue until the indicator changes from colourless to pink. Record the final burette reading in your results table.

   Step 8 Repeat the titration accurately by adding the acid drop-by-drop when you are near the end point.

   Step 9 Repeat the accurate titration until you have two concordant results.

   a. Complete the following diagram. [6]

   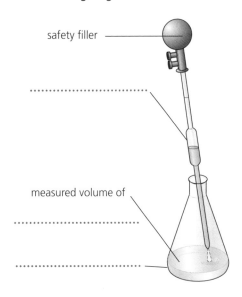
   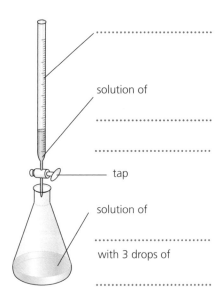

   safety filler

   measured volume of

   solution of

   tap

   solution of

   with 3 drops of

   b. Give the concentration of the sodium hydroxide that the student used in this titration.

   .... [1]

   c. In Step 9, 'concordant results' are mentioned. Describe what is meant by concordant results.

   .... [1]

d. The titration described in the method involves adding sulfuric acid to sodium hydroxide.

   i. Name the type of reaction that occurs in the conical flask.

   .... [1]

   ii. State the ions that cause a solution to be acidic.

   .... [1]

   iii. Suggest a pH for an acidic solution.

   .... [1]

   iv. State the ions that cause a solution to be alkaline.

   .... [1]

   v. Suggest a pH for an alkaline solution.

   .... [1]

e. Describe how to safely fill a burette.

....

....

....

....

.... [5]

f. Give the function of the white tile.

.... [1]

g. Describe **three** possible sources of error in this experiment.

....

....

.... [3]

h. State the correct position from which to read a value from a burette.

.... [1]

i. A titration stops when the end point has been reached. This is when all of the acid has been neutralised by the alkali.

   i. Describe how using an indicator can enable the student to tell when the end point has been reached.

   .... [1]

   ii. Suggest an alternative to an indicator that could also tell when the end point of a titration has been reached.

   .... [1]

2. A student carries out a titration between sodium hydroxide (NaOH) solution and dilute sulfuric acid (H_2SO_4).

   a. The student took a reading of 35 cm³ from the burette at the start of the experiment. Give this value in dm³.

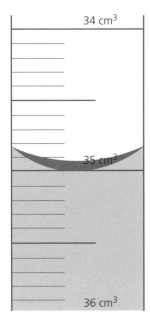

   .... [1]

   b. This figure shows the burette at the point when the solution in the conical flask turned pink.

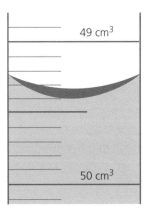

   Give the volume of dilute sulfuric acid that was required to neutralise the sodium hydroxide solution.

   .... [1]

   c. i. Write a balanced symbol equation for the reaction between sodium hydroxide (NaOH) solution and dilute sulfuric acid (H_2SO_4).

   ....

   .... [3]

ii. State how many moles of alkali react with 1 mole of acid.

.... [1]

iii. The student finds that 13.6 cm³ of 0.10 mol/dm³ sulfuric acid is required to neutralise 25 cm³ sodium hydroxide solution. Calculate the concentration of the sodium hydroxide solution in mol/dm³.

....

....

....

.... [6]

> **Exam tip**
>
> This is an example of how you could be asked to apply your maths skills in a practical context. Don't be put off by having to use knowledge from other parts of the Chemistry course.

d. The first time a titration is carried out the first result is called 'rough'.

i. Give the reason for finding a rough result.

.... [1]

ii. Complete the table by calculating the mean volume of dilute sulfuric acid needed to neutralise the sodium hydroxide. [1]

Trial 1 (rough)	Trial 2	Trial 3	Mean
17.10	16.35	16.30	

e. For a set of results to be concordant, they should be within 0.1 cm³ of each other. Suggest why concordant results are important when carrying out a titration.

.... [1]

3. A student uses the equipment shown to carry out a titration between sodium hydroxide solution and dilute hydrochloric acid. The conical flask has already been filled with 50 cm³ of 0.08 mol/dm³ hydrochloric acid.

a. Explain why a white tile is not needed in this version of the experiment.

....

.... [2]

The student plotted the following graph to show their results.

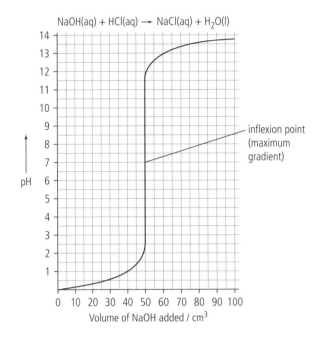

$$NaOH(aq) + HCl(aq) \longrightarrow NaCl(aq) + H_2O(l)$$

b. The student concludes that 50 cm³ sodium hydroxide is required to neutralise the hydrochloric acid. Give evidence from the graph that supports the student's conclusion.

.... [1]

Exam tip

There is 1 mark available, so you will only be expected to give one piece of information.

c. Calculate the concentration of the sodium hydroxide solution that the student used.

....

....

....

.... [5]

d. Calculate the mass of dilute hydrochloric acid that reacted with sodium hydroxide solution in this titration.

....

.... [2]

12 Solubility

1. A student is investigating this **solubility** of salts and draws this graph.

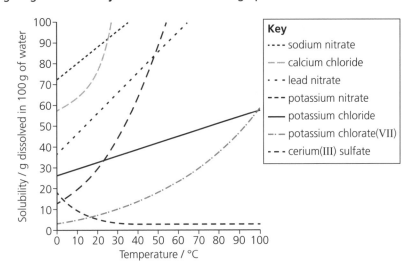

a. Use the student's graph to predict the most soluble salt at 20 °C.

.... [1]

b. Give the range of temperatures over which the student tested the salts.

.... [1]

c. Name the independent variable in this experiment.

.... [1]

d. Using lead nitrate as an example, state the conclusions that can be drawn from the graph.

....

.... [2]

Another student carries out a similar experiment but draws a different graph.

e. Name the independent variable in the second student's experiment.

.... [1]

f. Give the reason why the second student draws a bar chart and not a line graph.

.... [1]

g. State the conclusion that can be drawn from the second student's graph.

....

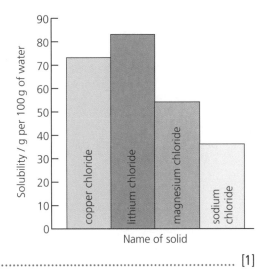

.... [1]

2. Limewater can be used to test for carbon dioxide.

   a. Give the positive test result that indicates the presence of carbon dioxide.

   .... [1]

   b. The chemical name for limewater is calcium hydroxide. When limewater reacts with carbon dioxide the products are calcium carbonate and water. Write a word equation for this reaction. Include state symbols.

   > **Exam tip**
   >
   > The state symbols are important here as most of the other information is given in the question.

   ....

   .... [3]

3. Silver nitrate can be used to test for the presence of halide ions which form insoluble precipitates.

   a. Describe what will be observed when a test for a halide is positive.

   .... [1]

   b. The different halide ions give positive results with similar colours. Suggest a way in which a student could be confident of the identity of the halide ion that gives a positive result.

   ....

   .... [2]

   c. Give a reason why barium chloride can be used to test for the presence of sulfate ions.

   .... [1]

   d. Either barium chloride or barium nitrate can be used to test for sulfate ions. A student has a sample in a test tube and needs to test this for both the presence of sulfate ions and the presence of halide ions. Describe how the test for sulfate ions should be carried out and state the order in which the tests for sulfate and halide ions should be performed.

   ....

   ....

   ....

   ....

   .... [5]

   e. Describe and explain the conditions needed for both the test for sulfate ions and the test for halide ions.

   ....

   ....

   ....

   .... [4]

1. A student has two white crystalline samples. They do not know their identity because the labels are missing. They decide to determine their identities by finding out how long it takes each substance to melt when heated.

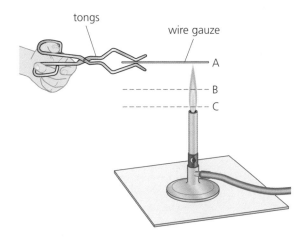

a. The student places each sample in a container on top of wire gauze above a Bunsen burner flame. Describe where the student should hold the gauze.

   ....

   .... [2]

b. Give **three** safety precautions that the student should take when carrying out this practical.

   ....

   ....

   .... [3]

c. Suggest the maximum time that each substance should be heated for. Explain your reasoning.

   ....

   ....

   .... [3]

d. The student finds out that one sample is a simple **covalent compound** while the other is an **ionic compound**. Complete this results table. [4]

	Sample	
	Sample 1	**Sample 2**
Time to melt / minutes	2 minutes	does not melt in 2 minutes
Ionic or covalent		

2. Two students use two different methods to determine the melting point of a solid.

Experiment 1

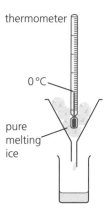

Experiment 2

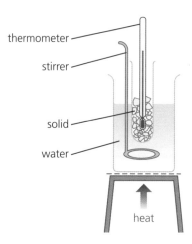

a. It is not possible to find the melting point of all solids by means of Experiment 1. Suggest a reason why.

....

.... [2]

b. Give the use of the stirrer used in Experiment 2.

.... [1]

c. Name the equipment that is used to measure the temperature in Experiment 2.

.... [1]

d. The ice in Experiment 1 is pure. Suggest a way to confirm this that does not involve measuring its temperature.

....

.... [2]

3. Very small samples of solids can be tested for purity using melting point analysis, using this equipment. This type of tube is called a Thiele tube.

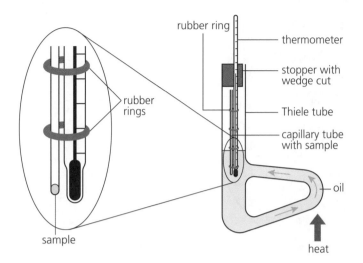

a. Suggest why the heat is not applied directly to the sample.

.... [1]

b. Explain why oil is used in the Thiele tube, instead of air or water.

....

.... [2]

c. Describe the result observed if a sample is pure.

.... [2]

d. Give a reason why the sample is contained in a capillary tube.

.... [1]

e. This experiment relies on visual inspection of the sample. Suggest an improvement to the method that will increase the accuracy.

....

.... [2]

4. This figure shows a fractionating column.

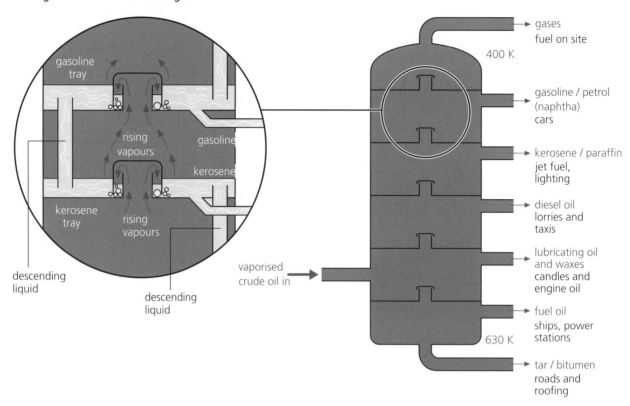

a. Describe how a mixture of crude oil is separated by **fractional distillation**.

....

.... [2]

b. Calculate the difference in temperature between the top and the bottom of the fractionating column.

.... [1]

c. Diesel boils at a temperature of 483 K. Give the condensing point of diesel.

.... [1]

d. Name the change of state that occurs as the fractionating column is ascended.

.... [1]

1. A student is comparing the reactivity of magnesium, zinc and copper.

   She adds magnesium sulfate solution to zinc and copper, zinc sulfate solution to magnesium and copper, and copper(II) sulfate solution to magnesium and zinc.

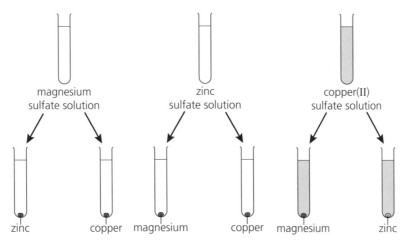

   a. The table shows the student's results.

	Magnesium sulfate solution	Zinc sulfate solution	Copper(II) sulfate solution
Magnesium	not tested	black precipitate	brown precipitate
Zinc	no reaction	not tested	brown precipitate
Copper	no reaction	no reaction	not tested

   Write the metals in order of reactivity, from most reactive to least. Justify your answer.

   ....

   ....

   .... [4]

   b. Name the type of reaction that is occurring in this investigation.

   .... [1]

   c. Suggest why magnesium sulfate was not reacted with magnesium.

   .... [1]

2. A student adds small pieces of zinc to a beaker containing copper(II) sulfate solution.

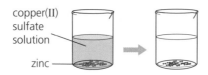

copper(II) sulfate solution

zinc

a. Write the symbol equation for the reaction that takes place in the beaker.

.... [2]

b. Describe what the student observes. Give a reason for each observation.

....

....

....

....

.... [5]

c. The student made their observations by eye.

Complete this sentence using the correct word in bold.

An observation made by eye is a **quantitative/qualitative** test. [1]

d. Suggest a method of carrying out this reaction that would allow measurements to be made and a graph to be drawn.

....

....

....

.... [4]

3. When chlorine solution is added to potassium bromide solution there is a reaction that causes a change in colour.

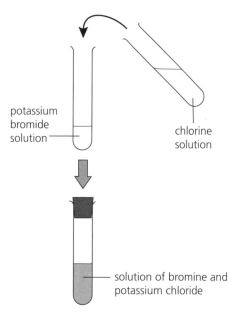

   potassium bromide solution

   chlorine solution

   solution of bromine and potassium chloride

   a. Explain why there is a reaction between chlorine and potassium bromide.

   ....

   .... [2]

   b. A student suggested that the same reaction would occur with chlorine solution and sodium bromide solution. Is this student correct? Explain your reasoning.

   ....

   ....

   .... [3]

4. Four new elements, W, X, Y and Z, have been discovered.

   Use the following data to work out the reactivity series of these elements. List the elements from least to most reactive.

	W sulfate solution	X sulfate solution	Y sulfate solution	Z sulfate solution
W metal	not tested	colour change seen	colour change seen	colour change seen
X metal	no reaction	not tested	no reaction	colour change seen
Y metal	no reaction	colour change seen	not tested	colour change seen
Z metal	no reaction	no reaction	no reaction	not tested

   .... [4]

1. A student is investigating the temperature changes when an acid is mixed with an alkali. They are given this method.

    Step 1 Place a polystyrene cup inside a 250 cm³ beaker.

    Step 2 Measure 30 cm³ of dilute hydrochloric acid in a measuring cylinder and pour it into the polystyrene cup.

    Step 3 Place a lid on the cup and insert the thermometer.

    Step 4 Record the temperature of the dilute hydrochloric acid.

    Step 5 Measure 5 cm³ of sodium hydroxide solution and pour it into the cup. Stir to mix.

    Step 6 Record the highest temperature reached on the thermometer.

    Step 7 Repeat Steps 5 and 6, adding 5 cm³ of sodium hydroxide solution at a time up to a maximum of 40 cm³.

    Step 8 Wash out the equipment and repeat Steps 1–7 two more times.

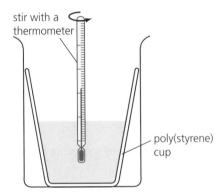

    a. State the purpose of:

        i. the polystyrene cup

        .... [1]

        ii. the beaker

        .... [1]

        iii. the lid.

        .... [1]

    b. Give **two** possible sources of error in this experiment.

        ....

        .... [2]

c. When recording temperature changes in this experiment, explain why it is important to wait until the reading on the thermometer stops changing and then to record the highest temperature reached.

....

.... [2]

d. The student carries out the experiment as stated in the method. He finds it difficult to measure the temperature accurately. Suggest equipment that can be used to obtain more accurate temperature readings.

....

.... [2]

e. There is no value given in the method for the time interval between adding each $5\,cm^3$ of sodium hydroxide solution to the hydrochloric acid. Suggest a difficulty that might arise if the sodium hydroxide solution is added:

  i. after very small time intervals

   .... [1]

  ii. after very long time intervals.

   .... [1]

f. In Step 8, the student is instructed to wash out the equipment and repeat the experiment.

  i. Give a reason why the experiment is repeated.

   .... [1]

  ii. Give a reason why it is important to wash out the equipment before it is used again.

   .... [1]

g. This reaction involves mixing an acid and an alkali. It is an example of a neutralisation reaction. Write the ionic equation for a neutralisation reaction.

   .... [3]

h. A student measures the energy change for a neutralisation reaction to be +41.7 kJ/mol.

  i. State whether energy is taken in or given out in this reaction.

   .... [1]

  ii. Name the type of reaction.

   .... [1]

2. A student carries out a **neutralisation** reaction between sodium hydroxide solution and dilute hydrochloric acid. She obtains the data shown in the table.

Volume of NaOH added / cm³	Mean highest temperature reached / °C
0	19
5	22
10	25
15	27
20	29
25	31
30	34
35	33
40	30

a. Use the student's data to draw a graph. Estimate a value for the highest temperature reached. You will need to draw **two** lines of best fit on your graph. [5]

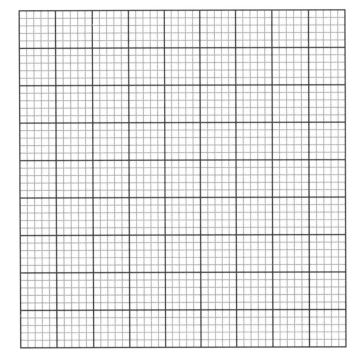

....

b. The student's data shows an upward and then a downward trend. Give reasons for these two trends.

....

....

.... [3]

c. Suggest a piece of equipment that would allow the maximum temperature to be recorded without having to draw lines of best fit on a graph.

.... [1]

d. Another student carries out the same neutralisation reaction by adding the sodium hydroxide solution in 5 cm³ increments. He draws a graph and estimates that the highest temperature change would be reached when he has added 23 cm³ of sodium hydroxide solution to the dilute hydrochloric acid. The student wants to obtain a more precise value for the highest temperature reached and the volume of sodium hydroxide solution at which this occurs. Explain how he can refine his method to obtain more precise results.

....

.... [2]

1. A student sets up four different test tubes to test the rate at which an iron nail rusts. Each nail is kept under different conditions.

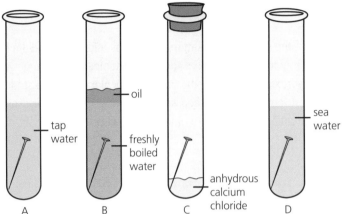

a. State the purpose of each different condition. Explain what the student is testing by using it.

   i. **A.** tap water

   ....

   .... [1]

   ii. **B.** freshly boiled water with oil on top

   ....

   .... [3]

   iii. **C.** anhydrous calcium chloride with a lid

   ....

   .... [3]

   iv. **D.** sea water

   ....

   .... [2]

b. Complete the results table for this experiment. Use the phrases: no rusting   some rusting   lots of rusting

	Condition/ Tube			
	Tube A. Tap water	Tube B. Freshly boiled water with oil on top	Tube C. Anhydrous calcium chloride with a lid	Tube D. Sea water
Result				

[3]

c. The student visually determines whether or not **rusting** takes place. Give the name of this type of test.

   .... [1]

d. The student suggests that setting up the experiment on a top-pan balance would make it easier to determine how much rusting has taken place. Explain how the balance would be used.

....

.... [2]

2. A student is investigating the rusting of iron wool using the equipment shown.

a. Suggest a reason why the student is using iron wool rather than a nail.

.... [1]

b. The level of rusting that occurs is determined by the movement of water up the test tube. Suggest an alternative piece of equipment that would allow the amount of rusting to be easily quantified.

.... [2]

c. The student uses tap water in the test tube. Suggest **two** ways in which the rate of rusting could be increased.

.... [1]

d. After one week, the water has moved up inside the test tube. Explain why this occurs.

....

....

....

.... [4]

3. A student wants to investigate how temperature affects the rate of **corrosion** of iron nails. They hang an iron nail from a thread, inside a test tube containing water, so that it is above the water level. They place a rubber bung into the neck of the test tube.

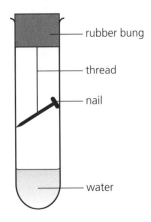

a. Give a reason why a bung is placed in the neck of the test tube.

.... [1]

b. The student determines the rate of corrosion by measuring the change in mass of the nail. Suggest a piece of equipment that is appropriate for this.

.... [1]

The student draws the following graph of their results.

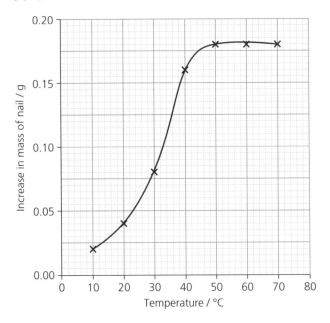

c. Give the range of temperatures over which the nail is tested.

.... [1]

d. Give the maximum increase in mass of the nail.

.... [1]

e. Calculate the rate of increase in mass at 20 °C. State the unit with your answer.

....

....

.... [3]

f. Explain why the mass does not increase after 50 °C has been reached.

....

.... [2]

g. The student then repeats the experiment with a new nail that has the same initial mass as the first nail. They use salt water instead of tap water in the test tube. Sketch a line on the same axes as above to predict the graph that the student obtains for their results. [2]

Anode The positive electrode in electrolysis.

Cathode The negative electrode in electrolysis.

Chromatography The separation of a mixture of soluble substances using filter paper and a solvent.

Chromatogram A piece of paper showing the separation of substances after chromatography has been carried out.

Cooling curve A graph showing how the temperature changes with time when a substance is cooled at a constant rate.

Control variable Any factor that is controlled or held constant during an experiment.

Corrosion The 'eating away' of the surface of a metal by a chemical, e.g. by acids.

Covalent compound A compound having covalent bonds. They can be simple molecules or giant structures.

Dependent variable The variable that is observed or measured in a scientific experiment. Dependent variables may change based on changes made to the independent variables.

Electrodes Rods that conduct electric current to and from an electrolyte.

Electrolysis The decomposition of an ionic compound when molten or in aqueous solution by the passage of an electric current.

Errors Errors can be random (usually the result of poor technique—not carrying out the experiment consistently) or systematic (consistent technique but repeating the error, such as inaccurate reading of a scale).

Fractional distillation A method used to separate two or more liquids with different boiling points from each other using a distillation column.

Independent variable The variable that is changed in a scientific experiment. Changing an independent variable may cause a change in the dependent variable.

Indicator A substance that has two different colours depending on the solution in which it is placed. It often changes colour according to the pH of the solution.

Ionic compound A compound having ionic bonds. Ionic bonds are strong electrostatic attractions between the positive and negative ions in the crystal lattice.

Ionic half-equation Equation showing the oxidation or reduction parts of a redox reaction separately. Often used for reactions at the electrodes in electrolysis.

Line of best fit Lines and curves of best fit should show an even distribution of points on either side of the line along its whole length.

Limewater A solution of calcium hydroxide in water, which is alkaline and turns milky in the presence of carbon dioxide.

Neutralisation The reaction between an acid and a base to form a salt and water.

Oxidation The loss of electrons or increase in oxidation number of a substance.

Oxidising agent A substance that accepts electrons and gets reduced.

pH Quantitative measure of the acidity or basicity of aqueous or other liquid solutions.

Precipitate A solid formed when two solutions are mixed.

Qualitative Qualitative data is descriptive information about characteristics that are difficult to define or measure or cannot be expressed numerically.

Quantitative Quantitative data is numerical information that can be measured or counted.

R_f The distance travelled by a substance during chromatography divided by the distance travelled by the solvent.

Rate of reaction The change in concentration of a reactant or product with time at a stated temperature.

Reducing agent A substance that reduces another substance by addition of electrons, and is itself oxidised in the process.

Reduction The gain of electrons or decrease in oxidation number of a substance.

Relative atomic mass The weighted average mass of naturally occurring atoms of an element on a scale where an atom of carbon-12 has a mass of exactly 12 units.

Rusting Corrosion of iron and iron alloys caused by the presence of both water and oxygen.

Saturated solution A solution which contains the maximum concentration of a solute dissolved in the solvent.

Solubility The amount of solute that dissolves in a given quantity of solvent.

Titration A method used to determine the amount of substance present in a given volume of solution of acid or alkali.

Key

| atomic number |
| atomic symbol |
| name |
| relative atomic mass |

Group

I	II	III	IV	V	VI	VII	VIII
							2 **He** helium 4
3 **Li** lithium 7	4 **Be** beryllium 9	5 **B** boron 11	6 **C** carbon 12	7 **N** nitrogen 14	8 **O** oxygen 16	9 **F** fluorine 19	10 **Ne** neon 20
11 **Na** sodium 23	12 **Mg** magnesium 24	13 **Al** aluminium 27	14 **Si** silicon 28	15 **P** phosphorus 31	16 **S** sulfur 32	17 **Cl** chlorine 35.5	18 **Ar** argon 40

1 **H** hydrogen 1

Transition elements:

19 **K** potassium 39	20 **Ca** calcium 40	21 **Sc** scandium 45	22 **Ti** titanium 48	23 **V** vanadium 51	24 **Cr** chromium 52	25 **Mn** manganese 55	26 **Fe** iron 56	27 **Co** cobalt 59	28 **Ni** nickel 59	29 **Cu** copper 64	30 **Zn** zinc 65	31 **Ga** gallium 70	32 **Ge** germanium 73	33 **As** arsenic 75	34 **Se** selenium 79	35 **Br** bromine 80	36 **Kr** krypton 84
37 **Rb** rubidium 85	38 **Sr** strontium 88	39 **Y** yttrium 89	40 **Zr** zirconium 91	41 **Nb** niobium 93	42 **Mo** molybdenum 96	43 **Tc** technetium –	44 **Ru** ruthenium 101	45 **Rh** rhodium 103	46 **Pd** palladium 106	47 **Ag** silver 108	48 **Cd** cadmium 112	49 **In** indium 115	50 **Sn** tin 119	51 **Sb** antimony 122	52 **Te** tellurium 128	53 **I** iodine 127	54 **Xe** xenon 131
55 **Cs** caesium 133	56 **Ba** barium 137	57–71 lanthanoids	72 **Hf** hafnium 178	73 **Ta** tantalum 181	74 **W** tungsten 184	75 **Re** rhenium 186	76 **Os** osmium 190	77 **Ir** iridium 192	78 **Pt** platinum 195	79 **Au** gold 197	80 **Hg** mercury 201	81 **Tl** thallium 204	82 **Pb** lead 207	83 **Bi** bismuth 209	84 **Po** polonium –	85 **At** astatine –	86 **Rn** radon –
87 **Fr** francium –	88 **Ra** radium –	89–103 actinoids	104 **Rf** rutherfordium –	105 **Db** dubnium –	106 **Sg** seaborgium –	107 **Bh** bohrium –	108 **Hs** hassium –	109 **Mt** meitnerium –	110 **Ds** darmstadtium –	111 **Rg** roentgenium –	112 **Cn** copernicium –		114 **Fl** flerovium –		116 **Lv** livermorium –		

lanthanoids

57 **La** lanthanum 139	58 **Ce** cerium 140	59 **Pr** praseodymium 141	60 **Nd** neodymium 144	61 **Pm** promethium –	62 **Sm** samarium 150	63 **Eu** europium 152	64 **Gd** gadolinium 157	65 **Tb** terbium 159	66 **Dy** dysprosium 163	67 **Ho** holmium 165	68 **Er** erbium 167	69 **Tm** thulium 169	70 **Yb** ytterbium 173	71 **Lu** lutetium 175

actinoids

89 **Ac** actinium –	90 **Th** thorium 232	91 **Pa** protactinium 231	92 **U** uranium 238	93 **Np** neptunium –	94 **Pu** plutonium –	95 **Am** americium –	96 **Cm** curium –	97 **Bk** berkelium –	98 **Cf** californium –	99 **Es** einsteinium –	100 **Fm** fermium –	101 **Md** mendelevium –	102 **No** nobelium –	103 **Lr** lawrencium –

Common ions

Monatomic cations

1+

H^+ hydrogen

Li^+ lithium

Na^+ sodium

K^+ potassium

Ag^+ silver

2+

Mg^{2+} magnesium

Ca^{2+} calcium

Ba^{2+} barium

Zn^{2+} zinc

Mn^{2+} manganese

3+

Al^{3+} aluminium

Monatomic anions

F^- fluoride

Cl^- chloride

Br^- bromide

I^- iodide

Polyatomic cations

H_3O^+ hydronium

Polyatomic anions

OH^- hydroxide

CO_3^{2-} carbonate

NO_3^- nitrate

SO_4^{2-} sulfate

$S_2O_3^{2-}$ thiosulfate

ClO_3^- chlorate

MnO_4^- permanganate

HCO_3^- hydrogen carbonate

Fe^{2+} iron(II) ferrous

Fe^{3+} iron(III) ferric

Pb^{2+} lead(II)

Cu^{2+} copper(II)

General equations

General salt equations

metal + acid → salt + hydrogen

metal oxide + acid → salt + water

metal hydroxide + acid → salt + water

metal carbonate + acid → salt + water + carbon dioxide

Neutralisation equation

$HCl + NaOH \rightarrow NaCl + H_2O$

Common simple molecules

NaCl

NaOH

H_2O

HCl

$Ce_2(SO_4)_3$

$KClO_3$

H_2SO_4

Na_2SO_4

$Ca(OH)_2$

$CaCO_3$

$MgSO_4$

LiCl

$CuCl_2$

$CaCl_2$

SO_2

$NaHCO_3$

$CuSO_4$

$Cu(OH)_2$

Answers

1 Simple quantitative experiments in chemistry

1. a. A
    b. i. $0.3\,cm^3$
        ii. Systemic error
        iii. $2.0\,cm^3$
    c. The reading is always taken from the top/consistent error
        It is the difference in volumes that is needed
2. a. $157\,cm^3$
    b.

Time / minutes	Volume of gas collected / cm^3
0	0
2	18
4	30
6	33
8	42
10	45
12	46

3. a. $84\,s$
    b. $72\,cm^3$
    c. i. $(120 - 40) = 80$
            $(24 - 8) = 16$
            $80 \div 16 = 5\,cm^3/s$
        ii. $104\,cm^3$

2 Rates of reaction

1. a. Volume of gas produced
    b. $2\,mol/dm^3$
    c. • volume of acid
        • length of magnesium ribbon
        • type of acid
    d. Any three
        • measuring loss of mass
        • colour change
        • production of product
        • turbidity of reaction mixture
        • change in pH
    e. To remove the layer of magnesium oxide
        so the magnesium can react immediately and there is no delay in the reaction
    f. Place a lighted splint into a test tube of the gas
        Hydrogen burns with a squeaky pop
    g. Mean rate of reaction = quantity of product formed ÷ time taken
    h. Mean rate of reaction = $56 \div 15$
        = $3.7\,dm^3/s$
2. a. $2.0\,mol/dm^3$ HCl will show the fastest rate and $0.5\,mol/dm^3$ will be the slowest
        The final volume of gas will be the same for each concentration
    b. i. Line with a steeper gradient
            Line levels off at the same volume of gas
        ii. More frequent collisions
            so a faster rate of reaction
            There is the same amount of each reactant so the same total amount of gas will be produced
3. a. i. Use of appropriate scales using more than half the available space
            All points plotted correctly
            Allow 1 mark for 4 points correctly plotted
        ii. Curved line of best fit
        iii. Tangents drawn on graph
            Rate is higher at 10 s
    b. i. Mean rate of reaction = decrease in mass of flask ÷ time taken
        ii. Mean rate of reaction = $(95 - 20) \div 40 = 1.875\,g/s$
        iii. Use of change in y / change in x determined from tangent
            Accept rate consistent with student's tangent on their graph
        iv. Reference to the relative formula mass of H_2 gas
            answer from 3b iii ÷ 2
4. a. This is a bad decision, as will cause an error in the results
        Different crosses will have different visibility
    b. $2HCl + Na_2S_2O_3 \rightarrow 2NaCl + S + SO_2 + H_2O$
    c. i. Solid; it will make it go cloudy
        ii. Aqueous
        iii. Gas; it starts to smell/bubbles appear
5. a. Different people have different levels of eyesight
    b. Different people will put the bung on the top at different speeds/times
6. a. Temperature
    b. A logger to measure the 'cloudiness' of the solution
    c. To keep the overall volume of the reactants the same
    d. 40 g of sodium thiosulfate has been dissolved in 1 litre of water

3 Salt preparation

1. a.

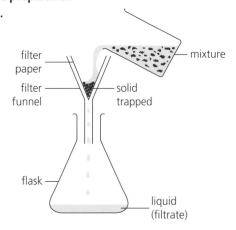

    b. Three from the following list. 2 marks per hazard, one for hazard and one for associated safety measure. 6 marks cannot be scored from just listing 6 hazards.

- Acid – can cause skin and eye damage – wash hands/eyes if it gets in contact and wear goggles/gloves
- Bunsen burner – can cause burns – inform teacher and keep burn under cold running water
- Glass – broken glass can cause cuts – inform teacher of any breakages, do not attempt to clear up yourself, seek first aid if required
- Copper sulfate – harmful if swallowed – inform teacher if swallowed and seek first aid

c. To remove the excess copper oxide/black powder

d. Leave sample on the window sill until next lesson/ heat directly (in a crucible)

e. To be able to get the salt out of solution

f. To make sure that all the sulfuric acid is fully reacted

g. 1 mole of CuO produces 1 mole of $CuSO_4$
   Relative formula mass of CuO is 79.5
   Relative formula mass of $CuSO_4$ is 159.5
   17 g of CuO produces $159.5 \div 79.5 \times 17 = 34$ g of $CuSO_4$

2. a. Gas A is hydrogen
   Test for gas A: It burns with a squeaky pop
   Gas B is carbon dioxide
   Test for gas B: It turns limewater cloudy

3. $CaSO_4$(s) is a solid
   The solution would go cloudy

4. a. Any suitable equation can gain marks for this answer.
      potassium + hydrochloric acid → potassium chloride + hydrogen
      potassium oxide + hydrochloric acid → potassium chloride + water
      potassium hydroxide + hydrochloric acid → potassium chloride + water
      potassium carbonate + hydrochloric acid → potassium chloride + water + carbon dioxide

   b. iron + sulfuric acid → iron sulfate + hydrogen
      iron oxide + sulfuric acid → iron sulfate + water
      iron hydroxide + sulfuric acid → iron sulfate + water
      iron carbonate + sulfuric acid → iron sulfate + water + carbon dioxide

   c. lead + nitric acid → lead nitrate + hydrogen
      lead oxide + nitric acid → lead nitrate + water
      lead hydroxide + nitric acid → lead nitrate + water
      lead carbonate + nitric acid → lead nitrate + water + carbon dioxide

4 Separation and purification techniques

1. a. A – filter paper
      B – residue
      C – filter funnel
      D – filtrate

   b. It can separate solid from liquid
      It cannot separate dissolved solid
      It cannot separate liquids

2. a. i. A solution with the maximum amount of dissolved solids at a given temperature
      ii. copper(II) sulfate
      iii. Change the temperature of the solution

   b. The size of the crystals will be different
      Fast evaporation of liquid using a Bunsen burner will lead to small crystals
      Slow evaporation by leaving on a window sill will lead to large crystals

3. a. • The Bunsen burner used for heating can cause burns.
      • The glassware will get hot; make sure it cools before you touch it.
      • Steam from the boiling mixture can cause scalds.
      • Wear eye protection.

   b. Water

   c. Measuring cylinder OR pipette OR burette

   d. To cool the liquid below its boiling point and condense the liquid

   e. A residue

   f. i. M_r of NaCl is 58.5
         M_r of $NaHCO_3$ is 84
         Sample A is sodium chloride
         Sample B is sodium hydrogen carbonate
      ii. pH meter/universal indicator paper

4. A detailed description of a method using correctly named distillation apparatus. Students should demonstrate that they understand that each fraction will evaporate separately depending on its boiling point and be collected separately.

5. a. If it was drawn in ink, the ink would run and this would give invalid results

   b. Below the origin line, so the samples aren't all dissolved in the solvent

   c. To stop the solvent evaporating

   d. So the results are not a mixture of different samples

   e. The middle of the spot

   f. Group A will have more accurate results
      Group B don't know where the solvent front is
      Group B can't calculate R_f values

   g. The sides of the paper will get wet which will change the path of the solvent front

   h. Qualitative
      It will tell the number of components and allow comparison, but will not give exact values on volume or mass

   i. A soluble sample would move but an insoluble sample would not move because an insoluble sample can't dissolve in the solvent

   j. From top:
      solvent front
      R_f value = 0.60
      R_f value = 0.34
      solvent

k. i. Blue
    ii. 3
    iii. C and E
    iv. A horizontal line drawn below the origin line
l. a. A and D
    b. i. R_f = distance moved by solute ÷ distance moved by solvent
        ii. R_f = 4.1 ÷ 8.6 = 0.48

5 Electrolysis

1. a. • 100 cm³ beaker
        • 2 × carbon electrodes
        • 2 × crocodile clips and wires
        • 1 × low voltage lab pack
        • copper(II) chloride solution
        • saturated sodium chloride solution
        • litmus paper
        • measuring cylinder
        • forceps
        • eye protection and nitrile gloves
    b. A short circuit
        Electrolysis will not take place
    c. 1 mark for risk and second mark for associated precaution, up to a total of 6. No more than 3 marks can be gained from listing risks only. One of the risks must refer to chlorine gas or copper chloride.
        Chlorine gas can be toxic – don't run the experiment for too long (5 minutes) OR work near an open window OR tell a teacher if you have breathing difficulties OR inform teacher if you're asthmatic
        Copper chloride solution is an irritant – inform teacher immediately if it gets into eyes or is swallowed, wash hands after use
        Broken glass can cause cuts – inform teacher of any breakages or cuts
        Spillages can cause accidents – clear up all spills
        Electricity can kill – follow a sensible working procedure the whole time – inform teacher of any broken equipment
    d. The same observations at each electrode, because they are using same reactants
        Different rate (speed) of reaction, due to different voltages
    e. Insert a bulb into the circuit to confirm that electricity is flowing through the circuit
    f. i. The cathode is the negative electrode
        ii. The anode is the positive electrode
    g. i. Negative (cathode)
        ii. Both are positive ions and are attracted to the electrode with the opposite charge
    h. i. Copper chloride
            Gas released: chlorine
            Test for gas: bleaches damp litmus paper
        ii. Copper sulfate
            Gas released: oxygen
            Test for gas: relights a glowing splint
    i. It forms a solid
        It gains 2 electrons
        It is reduced
    j. Sodium is more reactive than hydrogen
    k. NaOH
    l. Ions cannot flow in a solid
        The salt must be dissolved (molten is not a sensible answer and the temperature would be prohibitive)
    m. The solution becomes alkaline/the pH rises
    n. Oxidation is the loss of electrons; reduction is the gain of electrons (electrons must be in answer to gain marks)
    o. At the positive electrode (anode)
        $2Cl^- - 2e^- \rightarrow Cl_2$ or $2Cl^- \rightarrow Cl_2 + 2e^-$
        oxidation
        loss of 2 electrons
        At the negative electrode (cathode)
        $Cu^{2+} + 2e^- \rightarrow Cu$
        reduction
        gain of 2 electrons

6 Identification of metal ions, non-metal ions and gases

1.

Positive ion	lithium	sodium	potassium	calcium	copper
Flame test result	crimson	yellow	lilac	orange/red	green

2. Flame test
    Yellow flame indicates presence of sodium
    Addition of hydrochloric acid and barium chloride
    White precipitate seen indicates the presence of the sulfate ion
3. SO_4^{2-}
4. HCl
    HNO_3
5. Extinguishes a lighted splint
6. Splints soaked in solution or spray bottles
7. a. Copper(I) hydroxide
        Formula: CuOH
    b. Copper(II) hydroxide
        Formula: $Cu(OH)_2$
        Result with sodium hydroxide: blue precipitate
    c. Iron(II) hydroxide
        Formula: $Fe(OH)_2$
        Result with sodium hydroxide: green precipitate
    d. Iron(III) hydroxide
        Formula: $Fe(OH)_3$
        Result with sodium hydroxide: brown precipitate
8. The samples are contaminated with sodium OR the loop is contaminated OR the loop is not clean
    (yellow) colour for sodium masks all other colours
    Clean the loop in-between tests OR use a new loop

Answers

9. a. $CO_2 + Ca(OH)_2 \rightarrow CaCO_3 + H_2O$
   b. Calcium carbonate is a solid (precipitate)
10. a. $Ca^{2+} + 2OH^- \rightarrow Ca(OH)_2$
   b. With excess sodium hydroxide the white precipitate from aluminium hydroxide will dissolve whereas magnesium hydroxide will not
   c. Both will give a white precipitate with sodium hydroxide
   Calcium will give an orange/red flame, magnesium will not
11. Chloride ions will give a white precipitate
   Bromide ions will give a cream precipitate
   Iodide ions will give a yellow precipitate
   All results look very similar
   Use a reference set to compare unknown samples against
12. Testing for sulfate ions involves adding barium chloride
   These are the chloride ions that have tested positive with the halide test
13. a. Lithium chloride
   Flame test: crimson flame
   Halide test: white precipitate
   b. Sodium carbonate
   Flame test: yellow flame
   Test gas with limewater: turns limewater cloudy
   c. Copper sulfate
   Flame test or sodium hydroxide: green flame or blue precipitate
   Add hydrochloric acid and barium chloride: white precipitate
14. A is calcium carbonate, $CaCO_3$, B is magnesium sulfate, $MgSO_4$ and C is lithium chloride, LiCl

7 Chemical tests for water

1. a. Anhydrous copper sulfate
   b. Add water
   c. Anhydrous copper sulfate + water $\rightleftharpoons$ hydrated copper sulfate
2. Test the pH using universal indicator or pH meter
   Water will have a pH of 7
   Ethanoic acid will have a pH below 6
   Distil them
   Water will boil at 100 °C
   Ethanoic acid will boil at a different temperature

8 Test-tube reactions of dilute acids

1. a. Carbon dioxide turns limewater cloudy
   b. Water
   Salt/calcium chloride
2. a. Bubbles (gas)
   Magnesium will react very quickly
   Zinc will react slowly
   b. Hydrogen
   c. Burns with a squeaky pop

3. a.

	litmus	thymolphthalein	methyl orange
Expected result with acid	red	colourless	red
Expected result with alkali	blue	blue	yellow
Expected result with neutral solution	purple	colourless	yellow

   b. A neutral solution the same colour as one of the results
   c. Use universal indicator or a pH meter

9 Tests for oxidising and reducing agents

1. a.

Compound	Reducing agent	Oxidising agent
potassium iodide	✓	
nitric acid		✓
carbon	✓	
hydrogen	✓	
acidified potassium manganate		✓
oxygen		✓

   b. An oxidising agent
   c. The sample was a reducing agent
   The colour change was due to potassium manganate being reduced
   d. i. MnO_4^-
      ii. Mn^{2+}
   e. Colourless to brown

10 Heating and cooling curves

1. a. 7 minutes 45 seconds − 30 seconds = 7 minutes 15 seconds
   b. 100 °C
   c. It is pure
   It boils at a single temperature not over a range
   d. Thermometer or temperature probe
   e. 2 minutes 15 seconds to 7 minutes 15 seconds = 5 minutes

f. Very cold items can burn
Use gloves or tongs
Very hot items can burn
Stand back/use tongs/run hands under taps if burnt
Glass can break and cause cuts
Inform a teacher if glass is broken and ask them to clear it up
Spilt water can cause students to slip up
Clear up any mess immediately to prevent slip/trip hazards

g. Minutes allow a change to be seen without too many data points
Seconds would have too many data points to be able to take measurement accurately
Hours would be too long to show a change on a graph

2. a. Heating curve
b. 115 °C
c. Melting; because the compound is being heated
d. Add units to the *x*-axis

3. a. It is not water
It is solid at room temperature
b. Solidification/freezing
c. 53 °C

11 Titrations

1. a. Left-hand side labels:
pipette
measured volume of sodium hydroxide
conical flask
Right-hand side labels:
burette
solution of dilute sulfuric acid
solution of sodium hydroxide
with 3 drops of phenolphthalein
b. 0.100 mol/dm³
c. Within 0.1 cm³ of each other
d. i. Neutralisation
ii. H^+
iii. 1–6
iv. OH^-
v. 8–14
e. The tap must be closed (horizontal position)
Place a funnel in the top
Pour below eye level (e.g. place burette on floor)
Fill slowly so there is no overspill
Have beaker below to catch any drips
f. To enable any colour change be seen clearly
g. Bubble/air in tap
Not reading from the meniscus
Continuing to add acid beyond the end point
Misuse of pipette (wrong volume added to conical flask)

h. Bottom of the meniscus
i. i. The end point is shown by the first permanent colour change (answer must include permanent to gain marks)
ii. pH probe or data logger

2. a. $35 \div 1000 = 0.035\,dm^3$
b. $14.4\,cm^3$
c. i. $2NaOH + H_2SO_4 \rightarrow Na_2SO_4 + 2H_2O$
(1 mark for each product; 1 mark for correct balancing)
ii. 2
iii. $13.6 \div 1000 = 0.0136\,dm^3$ (volume of H_2SO_4)
$0.10 \times 0.0136 = 1.36 \times 10^{-3}$ moles H_2SO_4
$25 \div 1000 = 0.0250\,dm^3$ (volume of NaOH)
2 : 1 ratio so 2.72×10^{-3} moles of NaOH
$(2.72 \times 10^{-3}) \div 0.0250 = 0.109\,mol/dm^3$

d. i. To save time, run the majority of the solution through and only go drop by drop at the end
ii. $(16.35 + 16.30) \div 2 = 16.33$
e. For greater precision

3. a. The pH is measured by a probe
There is no colour change/no indicator
b. pH changes from acidic to alkaline (basic) at 50 cm³
c. $HCl + NaOH \rightarrow NaCl + H_2O$
1 : 1 ratio
Recognition that as volume the same and the ratio is 1 : 1, the concentrations will be the same
$0.08\,mol/dm^3$
d. $0.08 \times 0.05 = 4 \times 10^{-3}\,mol$
$4 \times 10^{-3} \times 36.5 = 0.146\,g$

12 Solubility

1. a. Sodium nitrate
b. 0–100 °C
c. Temperature
d. The solubility of a salt increases as the temperature of the water increases
e. The solid
f. The variable is discontinuous
g. Lithium chloride is the most soluble salt

2. a. The limewater turns cloudy
b. calcium hydroxide (aq) + carbon dioxide (g) → calcium carbonate (s) + water (l)

3. a. Goes cloudy/forms a precipitate/insoluble salt forms
b. Use ready-made known samples to compare results with
c. Barium sulfate is an insoluble salt
d. Barium nitrate should be used to test for sulfate ions as barium chloride will give a false positive result in the halide test
The test for sulfate ions should be done first:
silver from silver nitrate will give silver sulfate
silver sulfate is insoluble and will give a false positive result in the sulfate test

e. Acidified conditions:
name of a suitable dilute acid (e.g. HCl)
This removes carbonate ions as most carbonate ions are insoluble so may give a false positive result

13 Melting points and boiling points

1. a. B
The hottest part of the flame
b. Any three from:
wear goggles
stand well back
keep Bunsen burner away from edge of desk
use tongs
keep hands in cold running water if burnt
keep hair tied back
c. Under 5 minutes
This is enough time for a low melting point compound to melt – any longer may become dangerous (e.g. become too hot or release toxic fumes)
d.

	Sample	
	Sample 1	Sample 2
Time to melt / min	2 minutes	does not melt in 2 minutes
Ionic or covalent	simple covalent	ionic

2. a. The sample may ignite instead of melt
It may have a melting point below room temperature
b. To ensure an even distribution of heat
c. A thermometer
d. pH of 7
It does not conduct electricity
3. a. So that it is not overheated
To ensure even distribution
b. It is a better conductor of heat (than water or air)
c. It melts at a single temperature not over a range
d. The sample can be small
It is easy to see when the sample melts
e. A data logger/computer
To reduce bias or uncertainty
4. a. According to its boiling point
The hydrocarbon molecules form chains with different lengths which have different boiling points
b. 230 K
c. 483 K
d. Liquid to gas

14 Displacement reactions of metals and halogens

1. a. magnesium   zinc   copper
Magnesium reacts with both zinc sulfate and copper(II) sulfate so it is more reactive than both zinc and copper

Zinc reacts with copper(II) sulfate but not with magnesium sulfate so it is more reactive than copper but less reactive than magnesium
Copper does not react with either zinc sulfate or copper(II) sulfate so it is less reactive than both magnesium and zinc
b. Displacement reaction
c. No displacement could take place because the solution contains the same metal ions
2. a. $CuSO_4 + Zn \rightarrow ZnSO_4 + Cu$
b. The solid changed colour from black to brown
The solution changed colour from blue to colourless as zinc displaced the copper in the solution
The colour from copper sulfate was no longer seen because copper precipitated out of solution
c. Qualitative
d. Use a data logger or colorimeter which tests the absorbance of light at different time points
Compare with a reference curve of known concentrations
3. a. A displacement reaction occurs because chlorine is more reactive than bromine
b. No. Bromine solution would still be formed so the same colour change would still be seen
but sodium chloride would also be formed
4. Z
X
Y
W

15 Temperature changes during reactions

1. a. i. It is an insulator so it reduces energy loss to the surroundings
ii. To stop the polystyrene cup falling over
iii. To stop energy loss by convection from the top
b. There is transfer of energy to the surroundings
Errors in measurement of volumes/temperatures
c. A thermometer takes time to respond to temperature changes
The highest temperature needs to be recorded to improve the accuracy
d. A data logger/computer
This allows continuous monitoring/more accurate
e. i. If added too soon after previous volume of NaOH, the thermometer may not have finished responding to the first temperature change and inaccurate data will be recorded
ii. If the gap between the addition of NaOH is too long, the temperature of the solution may have started to fall due to energy loss before the reading is taken, which will lead to inaccurate results
f. i. To be able to spot anomalous results and calculate a mean

ii. To avoid left-over acid or alkali contaminating the next experiment, which will affect the results

g. $H^+ + OH^- \rightarrow H_2O$ (1 mark for each ion; 1 mark for water)

h. i. Taken in

ii. Endothermic

2. a. 1 mark for appropriate scale on *x*-axis

1 mark for appropriate scale on *y*-axis

1 mark for at least 7 of the points plotted correctly

1 mark for correct lines of best fit, both straight. One through the upwards data, one through the downwards data

1 mark for construction lines when working out temperature change

1 mark for temperature change in range 34.5–35.5 °C

b. The upwards trend is caused by bonds rearranging as neutralisation occurs

The temperature keeps going up until the reaction has finished

The downwards trend is due to the addition of cold liquid to hot liquid which causes cooling

c. A data logger

d. Repeat the experiment, focusing on the 20 – 30 cm³ range

Add the sodium hydroxide in smaller increments

16 Metals corroding

1. a. i. The control

ii. Boiling the water removes oxygen from the water

Oil stops oxygen entering the water

This tests whether the presence of oxygen affects rusting

iii. Anhydrous calcium chloride absorbs water from the air

The lid stops water entering

This tests whether the presence of water affects rusting

iv. Sea water contains salt

This tests whether the presence of salt affects rusting

b.

Condition/ Tube				
	Tube A. Tap water	Tube B. Freshly boiled water with oil on top	Tube C. Anhydrous calcium chloride with a lid	Tube D. Sea water
Result	Some rusting	No rusting	No rusting	Lots of rusting

c. Qualitative

d. Iron oxide will increase in mass because it takes in oxygen from the air

2. a. It provides a larger surface area

b. Use a measuring cylinder instead of a test tube

It allows readings of the water level to be taken

c. Add salt

Increase the temperature

d. Rusting had occurred

Rusting removes oxygen from the air

This decreases the pressure inside the tube

So the water moves upwards

3. a. To stop any more air entering

b. Scales/top-pan balance

c. 10 °C to 70 °C

d. 0.18 g

e. $(0.15 - 0) \div (60 - 6) = 0.003$ g/°C

Construction lines must be drawn on graph

f. The air in the test tube has been used up

g. Steeper line which ends at the same point 0.18 g

| Name: | Date: |

| Title: |

| Stage 1: Note observations | Stage 2: Formulate a question |

| Stage 3: Make a hypothesis | Stage 4: Conduct experiments |

| Stage 5: Record results | Stage 6: Report results |

Name:	Date:

Title:

Stage 1: Note observations	**Stage 2: Formulate a question**
Stage 3: Make a hypothesis	**Stage 4: Conduct experiments**
Stage 5: Record results	**Stage 6: Report results**

Name:	Date:

Title:

Stage 1: Note observations	**Stage 2: Formulate a question**
Stage 3: Make a hypothesis	**Stage 4: Conduct experiments**
Stage 5: Record results	**Stage 6: Report results**